W9-DCM-062

# GO FOR IT! ™

# WRESTLING
## START RIGHT AND WRESTLE WELL

OUR LADY OF PERPETUAL HELP SCHOOL
4801 Ilchester Road
Ellicott City, MD 21043

95-9838

## by Bill Gutman
## with Illustrations
## by Ben Brown

MARSHALL CAVENDISH
CORPORATION

GREY CASTLE PRESS

Marshall Cavendish Edition, Freeport, New York.

No part of this publication may be reproduced in whole or in part, or stored
in a retrieval system, or transmitted in any form or by any means, electronic,
mechanical, photocopying, recording, or otherwise, without written permission
of Grey Castle Press.

Published by arrangement with Grey Castle Press, Lakeville, Ct.

Copyright © 1990 by Grey Castle Press.

The *GO FOR IT* Sports Series is a trademark of Grey Castle Press.

Printed in the USA

The Library of Congress Cataloging in Publication Data

Gutman, Bill.
    Wrestling : start right and play well / by Bill Gutman ; with
illustrations by Ben Brown.
        p.    cm. — (Go for it!)
    Summary: Describes the history, current organization, including
teams, leagues, and championships, and techniques of wrestling.
    ISBN 0-942545-94-X (lib. bdg.)
    1. Wrestling—Juvenile literature. [1. Wrestling.] I. Brown,
Ben, 1921–    Ill. II. Title. III. Series: Gutman, Bill. Go for
it!
GV1195.G85    1990
796.8'12—dc20

89-7596
CIP
AC

*Photo credits:* Duomo, page 8, top and bottom, page 9.

*Special thanks to:* Fred Perry, varsity wrestling coach, Arlington High School,
LaGrangeville, N.Y.

*Picture research:* Omni Photo Communications, Inc.

## ABOUT THE AUTHOR

Bill Gutman is the author of over 70 books for children and young adults. The majority of his titles have dealt with sports, in both fiction and non-fiction, including ''how-to'' books. His name is well-known to librarians who make it their business to be informed about books of special interest to boys and reluctant readers. He lives in Poughquag, New York.

## ABOUT THE ILLUSTRATOR

Ben Brown's experience ranges from cartoonist to gallery painter. He is a graduate of the High School of Music & Art in New York City and the University of Iowa Art School. He has been a member of the National Academy of Design and the Art Students' League. He has illustrated government training manuals for the disadvantaged (using sports as themes), and his animation work for the American Bible Society won two blue ribbons from the American Film Festival. He lives in Great Barrington, Massachusetts.


In order to keep the instructions in this book as simple as possible, the author has chosen in most cases to use ''he'' to signify both boys and girls.

# A BRIEF HISTORY

**H**and-to-hand contests between men go back to the beginning of time. But no one can really say when wrestling began as a sport. Men sometimes wrestled in anger, if there were no weapons available. Or they might have been trying to find out which one was stronger.

It was almost natural that these hand-to-hand contests would become organized. Drawings from ancient cultures in such countries as Egypt and China show wrestling as a sport. And by the looks of the drawings, the wrestlers were using some of the same maneuvers as are used today.

In fact, drawings on the Beni-Hasan tomb in Egypt, made about 3,400 BC, show leg takedowns, headlocks and rides that look almost identical to those used by wrestlers today.

As early as 704 B.C., wrestling was part of the Olympic Games. Wrestling champions were treated as heroes in those days. But just when it looked as if wrestling would become a great ancient sport, there was a setback. It seems that wealthy people began betting on matches. And pretty soon wrestlers were being bought, often bribed to lose a match on purpose. That really marked an end to the first phase of the sport.

Believe it or not, it took many hundreds of years for wrestling to revive as a sport for all nations. It wasn't really until the nineteenth century that wrestling became popular once again. In the United States, it first became part of carnivals and circuses.

These traveling shows began putting on both freestyle and Greco-Roman matches. And because they stopped in so many towns and cities, wrestling began to become popular once again.

The first American champion was a man named William Muldoon in 1880. It finally looked as if the sport was here to stay. But then, after World War I ended in 1918, people started to "fix" matches again. Though this involved professional wrestlers, the entire sport was once more in question.

But in 1921, the Federation Internationale des Luttes Amateurs (FILA) was formed. It was this international body, formed to govern amateur wrestling, that really saved the sport. FILA not only set new standards and rules, but also organized and supervised nearly all amateur competition.

By 1924, there were seven freestyle weight classes and six Greco-Roman weight classes in the Olympics Games. Competition for the thirteen gold medals was fierce, with many countries sending wrestlers to compete. Today, there are ten Olympic weight classifications for each style of wrestling.

There are some basic differences between the freestyle and Greco-Roman forms of wrestling. Freestyle wrestling was once called "catch as catch can" wrestling. That meant there were no holds barred. It isn't quite that way anymore. There is certainly no punching, kicking, choking, or anything quite like that. But a wrestler can use his hands, arms, legs and feet to try to defeat his opponent.

In the Greco-Roman style, the legs cannot be used. That is, the legs cannot be used in creating or aiding in a hold. Nor can a wrestler apply a hold below the waist of his opponent. So the Greco-Roman style relies more on arm and upper-body strength.

Of the two forms of wrestling, freestyle is by far the more

6

popular in the United States. It is the style used in high school and college programs throughout the land. Colleges have been competing in the sport since the turn of the century, when Yale met the University of Pennsylvania in the first intercollegiate match. Most of the United States Olympic wrestlers participated in college programs.

Even though wrestling is a major college sport, it does not have a huge following among the general public. Far more people watch so-called "professional" wrestling. But professional wrestling is entertainment, rather than real sports competition. Yet when the word wrestling is used, many people think of Hulk Hogan instead of Dan Gable.

Dan Gable, however, was one of the most dedicated, single-minded athletes America has ever produced. Gable wrestled for the University of Iowa and was a collegiate champion. He was a man who just refused to lose. Many times his physical condition and will allowed him to defeat opponents with greater wrestling skills.

In the 1972 Olympics, Dan Gable had his greatest triumph. Going up against seasoned freestyle wrestlers from other countries, Gable won the gold medal in his weight class. Once more, he simply would not be beaten. He had worked harder than anyone and it paid off.

America has not had a lot of Olympic medalists in wrestling though. There have been only a handful since 1904, and none of them caught the fancy of the public like Dan Gable. After retiring as a wrestler, Gable returned to the life he knew best. He coached other wrestlers.

Dan Gable's Olympic triumph helped to increase interest in wrestling throughout the United States. By the 1984 Olympics, United States wrestlers were more than holding their own with the rest of the world. Two U.S. grapplers, light heavyweight

7

American heavyweight freestyle wrestler, Bruce Baumgartner, has the advantage over his opponent during the 1984 Olympic Games. Baumgartner went on to win the gold medal for the United States.

Jeff Blatnick in action during the 1984 Olympics. Blatnick not only defeated all his opponents. He also defeated Hodgkins Disease, a form of cancer, to pursue his wrestling dream.

Steven Fraser and superheavyweight Jeff Blatnick, became the first Americans even to take gold medals in Greco-Roman wrestling. In the same Olympics another American, Bruce Baumgartner, became the freestyle heavyweight champion.

Because wrestling is not a professional sport, it doesn't have a

**Bruce Baumgartner has his arm raised in victory as he wins Olympic Gold. Winning at the Olympics is perhaps the greatest goal of all amateur wrestlers.**

huge following among the public. But it is certainly drawing its share of fine athletes to compete at the top levels. The sport is demanding. A wrestler must be dedicated. He must be willing to make sacrifices. And he must want to excel at his sport.

There is no doubt that the sport is growing at the school and college level. It may not be as widespread as the so-called major sports—baseball, football, basketball—but wrestling programs are growing. Young people can also learn the sport at YMCAs or through wrestling clubs.

But it is the high schools and colleges that really develop the top flight competitors. Many fine colleges offer scholarships, as they do with other sports, and compete for the best wrestlers. And while the sport does not offer a lot of money and a pro career, there are still rewards.

A wrestler always has the satisfaction of knowing he has overcome his opponent. Besides winning a conference or NCAA championship, there is always the challenge of the Olympic Games. That means knowing you can compete with anyone in the world.

FILA is still the international governing body for amateur wrestling. The National Collegiate Athletic Association (NCAA) oversees the college sport. The United States Wrestling Federation, Canadian Amateur Wrestling Association and Amateur Athletic Union promote and conduct tournaments throughout North America. Strict guidelines for the sport at the high school level are set by the National Federation of State High School Associations. Matches are supervised by well-trained officials, with the safety of the wrestlers always in mind. Some 10,000 high schools throughout the United States now have wrestling programs for boys.

Wrestling has a long history. It's an ancient sport and a very basic one. Though wrestlers are members of a team, the sport is based on a one-on-one confrontation—man against man. No bats, rackets, sticks or other pieces of equipment. It's a unique challenge, and there are many young athletes who want to see if they can handle it.

# THE SPORT OF WRESTLING

**A** wrestling match takes place on a mat that is between two and four inches thick. On the mat is a circle not less than 28 feet in diameter. There is also a smaller circle in the center, 10 feet in diameter (for high school wrestlers). At the college level, the circle is in between 32 feet and 42 feet in diameter that serves as a starting point for the action. A safety mat wider than the large circle also surrounds the wrestling area. The safety mat can be rectangular or circular.

There are three ways to win a match. The first is to execute a *fall* or *pin*. That means pinning your opponent's shoulders flat to the mat. In high school wrestling, the pin must be held for two seconds. In a college match for one. A match can also be won at any time when one wrestler has achieved a 15-point lead over his opponent. This is called a *technical fall*. If there is no fall or technical fall, the winner is the wrestler who has scored the most points. There are a number of different ways points can be scored.

A match in high school consists of three, two-minute periods. In college wrestling, there is a two-minute period, followed by two, three-minute periods. And in the Olympics there are three, three-minute periods. Wrestling for the full amount of time at

12

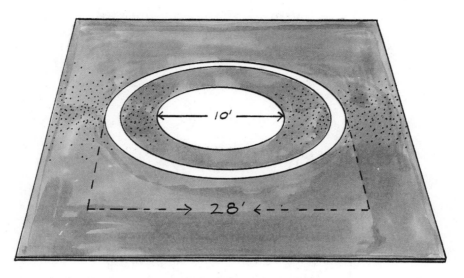

A wrestling mat is between two and four inches thick. The wrestling area is usually circular, 28 feet in diameter or less. There is also a safety area extending at least five feet beyond the circle on all sides. Inside the larger circle is a ten-foot starting circle. In the middle of this circle are two parallel starting lines (not shown), three feet long and twelve inches wide. One is red and the other green. These lines are used at starting points both for the neutral and referee's positions.

any of the levels is physically very demanding. A wrestler has to be in superb physical condition at all times. If he is unable to give one hundred percent effort throughout the match, there is very little chance of his winning.

Wrestlers are grouped solely by weight. In other words, a 200-pound wrestler is not going to go up against a 130-pounder. There can be a large variation in weight in the unlimited class, however. Even so, high school rules now provide a maximum weight of 275 pounds for heavyweights.

There are now 13 weight classes at the high school level. They begin at 103 pounds and go to 112, 119, 125, 130, 135, 140, 145, 152, 160, 171, 189 and unlimited to 275. These weight classes may vary from state to state.

College wrestling features 10 weight classes—118, 126, 134, 142, 150, 158, 167, 177, 190 and heavyweight. Finally, international

Wrestlers wear a one-piece uniform called a singlet. The high-top leather shoes have no heels. Also important is the headgear, which protects the wrestlers' ears. And don't worry. The smaller boy on the left won't have to wrestle the bigger boy on the right. Competition is by weight class only.

wrestling provides for eight different weights. They are 114.5, 125.5, 138.5, 154, 171.5, 191.5, 213.5 and heavyweight.

In some areas, high schools provide for a weight allowance as the season progresses. This is because young athletes are still growing. So by the end of the season, the high school weight limits are all three pounds higher than those listed above. The above weights, however, are the official ones.

A wrestler must always watch his weight very closely. The object is to wrestle in the lowest weight class possible, while maintaining maximum strength and endurance. That means if a young person in high school is wrestling at 122, he must keep his weight at 122 or below. If he weighs in at 123, he must either move up to the next weight class or not wrestle that day. If making a certain weight takes too much strength from a young wrestler, he should move up to the next weight class.

A wrestling match is divided into three periods. In the first, the two wrestlers face each other in a standing position. Each tries to get an immediate advantage by a takedown, which means forcing the opponent to the mat and taking control.

Starting positions for the second and third period are determined by a coin toss. The winner of the toss can choose the starting position for the second period. Then the loser chooses for the third period. The winner can also give the choice for the second period to his opponent and keep his choice for the final period. The wrestler can choose to begin again standing in the neutral position, or he can decide to start in the "referee's position," either on the top or bottom.

This means that the bottom wrestler has both his hands and knees on the mat. The top man then has the position of advantage. He is at the side of his opponent, but slightly behind him. He must put one arm around his opponent's waist and the other hand on his opponent's elbow. Some wrestlers prefer to start in the neutral position, others in the top referee's position, and still others in the bottom position.

Remember, a wrestling match ends any time there is a fall, no matter in which period it occurs. The match only goes to a decision if there is no fall. Even a wrestler way behind on points can win the match with a pin. It's similar to a boxer winning a bout by a knockout after trailing on points. So a wrestler should never be content to simply pile up points, unless he is close to winning by a technical fall.

There are a number of ways in which wrestlers can score points. Each takes a great degree of skill and knowledge of the sport. For as one wrestler is trying to make a scoring move, the other will try to counter it. Strength, speed, quickness, determination and stamina are all keys to winning.

Here, briefly, are the ways in which points are scored in a wrestling match. Two points are awarded for a *takedown*. A takedown occurs when both wrestlers are standing and one brings the other to the mat and then has control. One point is given for an *escape*, which occurs when one wrestler gets free from the control of the other.

Two points are also given for a *reversal*. This happens when a wrestler not only frees himself from the control of the other, but also gains control in the process. Another two-point maneuver is called a *predicament*. This occurs when one wrestler controls the other and the referee feels a fall or near fall may occur.

The *near fall* is worth two or sometimes three points. A near fall occurs when one wrestler pins one of his opponent's shoulders to the mat and holds the other shoulder near to the mat at an angle of less than 45 degrees. The near fall is worth two points if the shoulder is held at that angle for less than five seconds. It becomes a three-point maneuver is the shoulder is held close to the mat for more than five seconds.

**The object of any wrestling match is to hold your opponent's shoulders to the mat. This is called a pin or a fall. A pin is like a knockout in boxing. It ends the match immediately. If there is no pin, the match is decided on points.**

Those are the only ways points may be scored in high school wrestling. In the college version, points are scored the same way. But there is also one additional way to score. It is called a *time advantage* or *riding time*. One point is given for one minute of riding time, which means controlling your opponent for a total time of at least one minute.

Penalty points can also be given by the referee. They can be called for such violations as *stalling* or illegal holds. Either man can be called for stalling. The wrestler in control must continue to be aggressive and try to pin his opponent. He cannot be content to just hold his man down. By the same token, the wrestler on the bottom cannot just roll up into a shell so he won't be pinned. He must also be aggressive in his efforts to escape and take control of the match.

Wrestling, of course, is a highly individual sport. But there is also a team to consider. Wrestlers going in at different weight classes are representing their teams. And the overall object of the match is for the team to win. This, too, is decided by total points.

A team receives six points for a fall, a win by default, disqualification or forfeit. The last three are not that common. Five points are awarded for a technical fall. A match won by 12 or more points (but fewer than 15) is called a "superior decision" and is worth five points to the team. A match won by 8 to 11 points is a "major decision," worth four team points. A decision by fewer than 8 points is worth three points, and a draw counts two points for the team. Scoring can sometimes vary slightly from state to state.

The third man on the mat is the referee. He controls the match and awards all points. Because the sport is a hand-to-hand battle between two strong wrestlers, their safety is very important. The referee will make sure that all moves and holds are legal. If he sees an illegal or dangerous hold, he will stop the match by blowing his whistle and putting his right hand behind his neck. He will then award penalty points, if necessary, before restarting the match.

One illegal hold is to bend an arm or leg beyond the normal range of its movement. Another is a strangle or choke hold that prevents a wrestler from breathing. Still another is a *head scissors*, or holding the head between the feet or legs. If the ref sees any illegal hold that could cause an injury, he will stop the match immediately.

And, of course, things such as pulling hair, punching, gouging and kicking are not allowed. Nor is grabbing the end of the mat for leverage.

There are many different kinds of holds and maneuvers a wrestler can use to gain an advantage and score points. Some of these moves involve tripping, tackling, lifting, throwing and twisting. But with so many holds, very few wrestlers can learn them all. It's better for a young wrestler to learn to use his strengths. He should work on the maneuvers that suit his size, strength, speed and build. These will become the basic things he can rely on in a match.

Then, as a young wrestler gains experience, he can begin adding to the number of things he does well. It's better to be able to execute a certain maneuver very well than to have five maneuvers that he can do only fairly well. The more wrestling experience he has, the better wrestler he will become.

# Uniform And Equipment

There is really not much equipment involved in wrestling. The uniforms are standard and very basic. The uniform itself is called a "singlet." It's just one piece, a combination of shorts and shirt with shoulder straps. Many wrestlers or teams also wear full-length wrestling tights under the singlet.

Shoes are generally made of lightweight nylon and leather. They have no heels and come up above the ankle. The only other piece of equipment is the headgear, made of lightweight plastic or similar type material.

In the old days, you could always tell a wrestler by his ears. Many had what is called a "cauliflower ear." The ear was actually deformed from being pushed and rubbed on the mat. Today's wrestlers wear a special piece of headgear designed to protect the ears. It covers only the ears with a triangle-shaped piece and is held on by three straps. One is a chinstrap, the other goes over the top of the head and the third behind the head.

Wrestlers should always be sure that shoes and headgear are in tip-top shape. But other than that, they don't really have to worry about their equipment. In fact, you might say that the wrestler's most important piece of equipment is his own body. He must care for it constantly, as much or more than any other type of athlete. Wrestling is a sport in which a single pound can make a difference. So it's a fine line and the wrestler must learn to walk it carefully.

# Getting Ready To Wrestle

Wrestling is a sport that demands total dedication throughout the season. If you have that, you will work hard in the off-season as well.

It's important to realize something about wrestling right away. Even though it is a team sport, when a wrestler comes out for his match, he's all alone. He must give everything he has against his opponent. That can mean all-out wrestling for six to eight minutes, depending on the level.

Baseball, football or basketball are all team sports. Sometimes you can hide in the crowd if you're not having a good day. Your teammates can pick up the slack, or you can even leave the game for a while. But in wrestling, you cannot afford to have a bad day.

A wrestler cannot go out onto the mat with a case of the blahs. He can't say he just doesn't feel like wrestling. Because if he goes out feeling that way, he is likely to find his shoulders on the mat very quickly. So every single time he gets set to face an opponent, he must be ready to wrestle. And that means giving a complete effort for the entire match.

Any beginning wrestler must start with conditioning. He must work on both strength and stamina. For if a wrestler tires before his opponent, he will almost surely lose. He may also have fine technique. But if he doesn't have the strength to use it, the results will not be good.

Wrestling has been described as six or eight minutes of all-out activity. There is no way around that. Each competitor must be prepared to go the full distance every time. In addition, today's athletes are very well trained. Fewer wrestlers than ever are winning, if they have only average strength. A wrestler must expect that every opponent is going to be quite strong for his weight. So he must be prepared to match strength, as well as skill.

Building up stamina begins with running. All wrestlers should have a regular running schedule, which they should follow throughout the entire year. By running long distances (two to five miles) several times a week, they will slowly increase their stamina. It's also a good way to help keep any excess weight from building up.

In addition to distance running, a wrestler can also do wind sprints. A good workout is to run all out for maybe 15 or 20 yards, turn, then sprint back the same distance. Keep doing this until you feel you are exhausted. Then do a few more! The wind sprints will help you when you need a sudden burst of energy during a match. They will also help build character by teaching you that you can always do one more—even when you think you can't.

Of course, once you begin to wrestle, your workouts with your own teammates will also help you to build stamina and become match tough. There is often fierce competition among teammates to win the one position in each weight class.

While a wrestler is building endurance and stamina, he must also be building his strength. There are two kinds of strength necessary for a wrestler. The first, of course, is just power. That is the ability to move your opponent by being as strong or stronger than he is. The second kind of strength is staying power. That is the ability to move that opponent as easily in the final minute of the match as in the first minute.

A vigorous program of exercises is also very good for the wrestler. This can include push ups, pull ups, sit ups, parallel bar dips and squats. These exercises, done one right after another, will help with both strength and stamina. Some coaches even encourage rope climbing, which builds up your hands, arms, shoulders and back.

But more and more of today's wrestlers are depending on some form of weight training. In fact, it's hard to picture a wrestler today who doesn't lift weights to some degree. Otherwise, he just won't be strong enough. But remember, any kind of weight program should be done under supervision. Find a coach who knows your goals and follow the program he maps out for you.

Two general styles of weight lifting are usually suggested for wrestlers. Remember, you are trying to build both power and endurance. Power comes from using heavy weights and repeating the exercise a few times. Endurance comes from using lighter weights but repeating the exercise many times. The number of times an exercise is repeated is called repetitions or "reps."

A coach will generally outline both types of lifting—high weight, low reps for power, and low weight, high reps for endurance. For example, an exercise with a heavy weight might call for one set of three to ten reps. A set, by the way, is a group of reps.

On the other hand, an endurance type exercise might call for three sets of 15 reps each. That means you would repeat the exercise 15 times, rest, then do another 15. After another short rest period, you would do 15 more reps of the same exercise.

Anyone lifting weights should remember to work with the whole body. Some wrestlers tend to work so hard on their arms and shoulders that they neglect their legs. It's true that the legs aren't as important in wrestling as in some other sports. But

**All wrestlers today find it necessary to train with weights. Maximum strength is very important to a wrestler. It takes this kind of strength to execute many of the holds and maneuvers. A good coach is essential when a young wrestler begins to work with weights.**

they should still not be neglected when it comes to body building.

Wrestlers generally weight train all year round. Before and after the season, they work out two or three times a week. During the season, it's usually once a week. The weight work during the season should be mostly the low weight, high reps type. The trick during the season is not to build strength, but to maintain it. Without any weight lifting at all, the wrestler's strength will fall off to some degree during the year as he competes.

Weight work should not be done, as a rule, within 24 to 48 hours before a match. It takes that long for the muscle fibers to build up again after a hard workout. So to lift just before competing might well cause a temporary loss of strength.

**When doing an exercise such as the bench press, always have two "spotters" to help give you the weight and take it away. To try to do an exercise like this alone can lead to serious injury.**

Your weight work can be done with free weights (the old fashioned barbells) or with the new weight machines that are now in many exercise rooms. Always try to work with someone else, never alone. When you work with free weights, always have someone spot for you to avoid a possible accident.

Perhaps the most important thing a young wrestler should worry about is his weight. For years, it was felt that a young person should wrestle at the lowest weight possible, if he could maintain his strength. This is where a good coach is important. A young athlete should never try to cut his weight to an unnatural level just to wrestle.

Every boy must remember that he is going to gain weight as he grows. This will happen whether he works out or not. So once he makes a commitment to wrestling, his weight will always be a concern. The low weight theory is as follows. Suppose a young wrestler starts out as a natural 145 pounder. If he can maintain his strength, he would probably have a better chance to win by wrestling at 138. So he is asked to drop seven pounds.

With some wrestlers, this can work. Perhaps they have a little body fat and actually work it off as they get stronger. Then dropping to a lower weight class is fine. But if the boy is forcing the weight off by not eating, or by taking diuretics (drugs that cause a loss of body fluid), then he is only hurting himself and his team.

A good coach will not force his wrestlers to cut weight. If he sees a boy can no longer make 138, he will allow him to wrestle at 145. It may be tougher for the young person at the higher weight class, but it will be healthier. Some coaches, in fact, feel that their wrestlers might be better off at a higher weight class. They will learn more that way, and maybe even improve by wrestling someone a few pounds heavier.

Young wrestlers right through high school should not make

an off-season decision to lose weight. Don't say in the summer that you've got to wrestle at 138 the next winter. Remember, you're growing and if you are lifting weights, you are also putting on muscle. Come back to school at your natural weight and then take the advice of your coach.

But a wrestler should watch calories. He should eat a healthy diet. It should be a diet, however, in which fresh fruits and vegetables are more important than milk shakes and french fries. By the same token, smoking, drinking and any kind of drugs are out for a wrestler. The sport is just too demanding.

One more word about getting ready. Determination and will make up a big part of wrestling. A wrestler who goes out on the mat thinking he cannot win, won't win. So you must approach each match with confidence. You must think positively. You must feel you can win right up to the final whistle.

Once you sense your opponent has let down during a match, you must go after him. Be aggressive. Try to get a psychological advantage. If a wrestler gives up, his opponent will sense it. If a wrestler is just trying to last the eight minutes, his opponent will sense it. Once you give up, you've lost. Many matches have been won in the final period by a wrestler who has confidence and determination. Even if he is losing on points, he keeps trying to win.

Although wrestling is not an easy sport, it can be a very satisfying one. It's a sport that builds self-confidence and self-esteem. It will also leave you with both a healthy mind and healthy body. If you feel you want to try it, go for it. Just make sure you get ready the right way.

Note: Because freestyle wrestling is so much more widely practiced than Greco-Roman, the following sections all refer to freestyle wrestling only.

OUR LADY OF PERPETUAL HELP SCHOOL
4801 Ilchester Road

# LEARNING HOW TO WRESTLE

## Learning Takedowns

Every wrestling match begins with the two wrestlers on their feet and facing one another. Each will try to score the first points by taking the other to the mat. There are a number of different ways to try for the takedown. It's an important skill not only for the beginning of the match, but also later. If there is an escape at any time, the wrestlers may find themselves facing each other again. So the takedown becomes very important.

Balance and momentum are especially useful in the takedown. Because of an opponent's balance, as well as his speed and technique, the stronger wrestler doesn't always win.

Whenever a wrestler is on his feet facing an opponent, he must take the basic ready stance. It will allow him to move quickly in any direction. There are two similar stances—the *square stance* and the *staggered* or *lead-foot stance*. With the square stance, both feet are even, slightly wider than shoulder width. The knees are bent, the back is straight, and the wrestler's head is up, with hands out in front and ready. The elbows should be tucked in close to the body.

The staggered stance is the same, except that one leg is placed about 18 inches in front of the other. Both stances will get the

This is the basic ready stance a wrestler uses when squaring off against an opponent. Knees are bent, back held straight, hands are out in front of the body with the elbows tucked in close. Pictured here is the staggered, or lead foot, stance. With this stance, the wrestler keeps one foot in front of the other. Some prefer the square stance with both feet even.

job done. Which one you use depends on which feels more comfortable. It might be a good idea to point your toes slightly outward, too. This can help with balance. Some wrestlers will also flex their knees in the ready stance. They feel that the repeated up-and-down body movement helps them.

Of course, there are many ways a wrestler can attack an opponent when trying for a takedown. We can't talk about them all, so we'll just look at some of the basic ones.

As you move around the mat, you are looking for an advantage. Always watch your opponent carefully. Don't watch his head or eyes. That will make it easier for you to fall for a fake. Instead watch the movement of his legs. That way, you can tell right away how his body is going to move.

The aggressive wrestler will try to set up his opponent for the takedown. This means making him react to something you are doing. It could be a faking move, as if you are going to dive for his legs. (Making a quick move for the legs is called "shooting.")

Or a reaching move, as if you want to grab an arm. This kind of feinting and faking could put him off balance. And that is what you are looking for.

Set ups also involve touching or grabbing your opponent. You are allowed to grab and tap him, looking for an opening. Some wrestlers prefer to go for a *tie-up*. That means grabbing the opponent by the arms, wrists, or around the back of the neck with your hand. Once you have a hold, you can look for an opening to try a takedown move.

But most wrestlers prefer a fast, decisive move. This initial move is called *penetration*. It means penetrating your opponent's defense by driving toward him. This first move should be so

*Left.* The double-leg takedown begins with both wrestlers squaring off in the ready position, looking for an advantage. Wrestlers will often jab, tap or grab an opponent, trying to set up that first decisive move. *Right.* With the double-leg takedown, the wrestler on the left has taken a long step with his right leg, putting his foot between the feet of his opponent. The strong, shooting move will result in his lead knee coming to the mat as he locks both his arms around the thighs of his opponent. As with all wrestling moves, explosive speed and power are needed to make the move successful.

strong that you are actually trying to drive through him to a spot behind him. If penetration results in contact and you want to pick your man up, be sure to use your legs and back.

If your penetration results in contact with his thighs, you should hit hard, then straighten and lift your opponent off the mat. It could result in a takedown. In fact, this kind of maneuver could lead to a *double-leg takedown*, which is one of the basic takedown maneuvers.

The double-leg takedown begins with a deep, or long, lead step. You must penetrate enough to get your foot between your

Once his right knee is on the mat, the wrestler begins to lift his opponent off his feet. To get better leverage he must bring his trailing foot forward and place it on the mat even with the lead knee and a shoulder's width away. The object is to drive him over his shoulder and then take him to the mat. This is where strength helps. An opponent never goes easily. He is always resisting or trying a countering move. So strong, quick movements are very important.

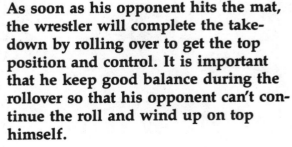

As soon as his opponent hits the mat, the wrestler will complete the takedown by rolling over to get the top position and control. It is important that he keep good balance during the rollover so that his opponent can't continue the roll and wind up on top himself.

opponent's feet. Then follow through with the move. Bring your lead knee to the mat and lock both arms around your opponent's thighs. When your knee hits, you are ready to lift him off the mat. You can drive him over your shoulder and back to the mat. Then as soon as he hits the mat, roll over to get the top position. Always spread an arm for balance, so he cannot keep you moving and roll right over you.

A variation of this move is the *single-leg takedown*. It is perhaps the most basic of all takedown moves. This time, the deep step is taken toward the outside of one of his feet, not between. As your lead knee hits the mat, hook your arm behind his knee. Then, as you pivot with the knee that's on the mat, you'll drive

*Left.* A similar takedown maneuver is the single-leg takedown. This one begins with the wrestler taking a deep step toward the outside of one of his opponent's feet. Just as his knee heads down to the mat, the wrestler hooks his arm behind his opponent's knee. *Right.* Next he pivots around his opponent on the knee that is on the mat. As he does so, he drives his shoulder into the back of the other wrestler's leg. This maneuver should buckle the leg and allow the wrestler to bring his opponent to the mat to complete the takedown.

your shoulder into the back of his leg. His knee should buckle, enabling you to bring him down to the mat.

The *high-crotch takedown* is a maneuver that relies on quickness and strength. It generally starts from an *elbow tie up*. If your opponent grabs the side of your neck, you counter by grabbing the elbow of the arm he has extended. Always keep your thumb to the outside of the elbow.

Now move fast. Push his elbow inward toward his body. As he starts to react, suddenly pull the elbow out again and take a

*Left.* The high-crotch takedown is another maneuver that takes a combination of speed and strength. It usually begins with an elbow tie up. The wrestler on the right has moved to control his opponent's right elbow after the opponent has grabbed him by the neck. Notice that the wrestler on the right has grabbed his opponent's elbow with his thumb on the outside. *Right.* Still controlling his opponent's elbow, the wrestler has to move fast. First he pushes the elbow in toward his body. But as his opponent begins to react, he suddenly pulls it away again and at the same time takes a deep step with his outside leg. With his foot between his opponent's feet, he will drop down low and reach between his legs with his free arm.

*Left.*  Next, he will drop to his knee and control his opponent's weight with his shoulder and arms. At this point, the wrestler is still holding his opponent by the elbow and also behind the leg. *Right.*  To complete the takedown, the wrestler releases his opponent's elbow and pivots quickly on his knee. Looking over his right shoulder, he swings his free arm over his opponent's waist. This should enable him to finish pivoting and at the same time drive his opponent to the mat. Then he will have a takedown and will be in a position of control.

deep step with your outside leg. The stepping foot will be between his feet. Then drop to your knee, reach under and place your free arm between his legs, high in the crotch. Keep your back straight and your head up.

As he tries to brace himself, you must pivot quickly on the knee that is on the mat. Then look over your shoulder and swing your free arm behind his hips. This should allow you to knock him to the mat and roll over into a controlling position.

The *duck-under takedown* begins the same way as the high crotch takedown. You have your opponent's elbow with one arm, while the other arm is in a *collar* or *neck tie up*. What you must do is lift the opponent's arm by the elbow, then lower

32

*Left.* The duck-under takedown also begins with an elbow tie-up (not shown). Only this time when you raise your opponent's elbow away from his body, you quickly duck under his raised arm by taking a deep step with your outside foot. Remember to keep your back straight and head up and you make the duck-under. *Right.* With your stepping leg outside your opponent's hip, quickly pivot around behind him. You are now controlling him from behind and should be able to drive him forward to the mat to complete the takedown.

your body at the knees. Keep your back straight and head up as you duck under the raised arm by taking a deep step with your outside leg. With your leg outside your opponent's hip, you can now pivot around behind him and knock him to the mat for a takedown.

The *arm-drag takedown* also involves stepping around the side of your opponent. To begin the arm drag, you've got to grab your opponent's wrist. You have to control this move by sliding your thumb and forefinger down to the groove between the forearm and hand. Then squeeze hard. Strength again.

Next reach across with your free hand and grab the elbow of the arm you're already controlling. As you release his wrist, pull

*Top.* To begin the arm-drag take-down, you must grab your opponent's wrist with your hand (not shown). Then pull his arm across your body so you can grab his elbow with your other hand. At the same time, take a deep step toward him, putting the stepping foot right between his feet. *Middle.* Next, begin to pivot on your lead foot, swinging your outside leg and outside arm behind your opponent. Like all takedown moves, this one must be made quickly and explosively. *Bottom.* Complete the takedown by using your knee to hit your opponent's knee from behind. That should buckle his leg. If you also pull down with the arm around his waist, you should drive him to the mat and finish almost in the referee's position, as pictured here.

the elbow across the front of your chest. Then take a lead step that will place your foot between your opponent's feet. Next, pivot on that foot and swing your outside leg and arm around the side and behind your opponent. You can complete the takedown by hitting him behind his knee with your knee, while also pulling him with your outside arm around his hip.

There are a couple of takedown maneuvers that rely as much on strength as they do on quickness. One is the *bearhug*. This is a favorite of very strong grapplers. It is an upper body attack in which the wrestler takes a deep step into his opponent and wraps both arms around his torso. He can now throw his opponent sideways to the mat or can drive him backward and try to cave him in.

The *headlock* is another basic takedown that uses pure power. The attacker simply gets close enough to wrap an arm around his opponent's head. He then can force his opponent straight down or throw him off to the side.

All these takedown maneuvers, as well as others, will work if executed well. But a wrestler must remember that there are counter moves. A good opponent who sees a certain maneuver coming can move quickly to counter it. Either the takedown won't work or the opponent will get a takedown of his own.

That's why a wrestler cannot depend on just one or two good takedown moves. He must learn several and be able to execute them. Then, as he gets more experience, he can begin adding to the number of moves he can make. The following are some basic tips that will help you with your takedown technique.

Remember to never look your opponent in the eyes. You can best tell what he plans to do by watching his legs. When you make a move, make it decisive. Don't stop and pause in the middle. Let takedowns be explosive and smooth. Learn to make your takedown moves from both the left and right sides. Never cross your legs when moving about the mat. And after a takedown, always try to follow with a pinning move.

The better a wrestler is at takedowns, the better start he will get in a match. It's almost like scoring the first run in baseball or the first touchdown in football. In fact, statistics show that the wrestler who gets the first takedown will win the match 90 percent of the time.

So work hard on your takedown techniques. Listen to your coach and practice. That's the key. With any kind of wrestling move, you've got to work with a live opponent. Only then can you become better.

Before leaving takedowns, just a word about *counters*. A counter is a move that will stop the offensive maneuver of an attacker. In addition, a good counter can lead to an advantage by the wrestler making it. There are many counter moves in wrestling. Here we will mention just a few so that the meaning of the counter is clear.

If a wrestler goes for a single-leg takedown, his opponent can counter, if he is quick enough. It is done simply by spreading the legs backward, putting them out of reach of the attacker. At the same time, the defender can use his arms to press down on the head and shoulder of the attacker. This way, he has a chance for a takedown of his own.

The duck-under takedown can also be stopped if the opponent is quick enough. He can do this by catching the head or arm of the attacker as he is ducking under. If he does that, he can turn it into an advantage and maybe a takedown.

Any good coach will undoubtedly know a counter for nearly every attack. So there is a lot to learn. A good coach and experience are the best teachers.

36

# Learning Escapes And Reversals

The last two periods of a wrestling match begin with the wrestlers in the referee's position. The bottom man has both hands and knees on the mat. The top man kneels alongside but slightly behind his opponent. He places his left hand on the bottom man's left elbow and his right arm lightly around his opponent's waist. So the top man has the immediate advantage.

What the bottom man must do is try to escape. If he can break free, he not only gets one point, but ends up facing his opponent from a standing position. He has taken away the advantage from the top man.

Some coaches feel that a wrestler should pick the top position if he wins the coin toss before the second period. The reason for this isn't simply because he will start on top. It is because the wrestler starting on top in the second period will be the bottom man for the third. And many feel it's easier to score points from the bottom position, with an escape or reversal.

By the third period, a wrestler will know just how many points he needs to win. If he is in top physical condition, starting the final three minutes of wrestling in the bottom position isn't such a bad idea.

Now for a few escapes. Perhaps the most basic escape maneuver from the bottom position is the *stand-up*. If done right, the stand-up will put the down man right back in a standing, neutral position. To execute the stand-up, the bottom man must remember to secure hand control on the way up and to keep his back straight, head up and knees bent. Otherwise, his opponent may lift him up and throw him back down as soon as he reaches a standing position.

You begin the *inside-leg stand-up* by stepping up with your in-

*Upper Left.* One of the basic escapes from the bottom starting position is the inside-leg stand-up. The bottom wrestler must make his move in a quick and explosive way. Because the top wrestler wants to keep control, he will be ready to counter almost any move. *Upper Right.* The bottom man begins the stand-up by actually stepping up with the inside leg. Once his foot is on the mat, the wrestler takes his inside arm and turns the palm up. He will then jam his elbow back toward his opponent. This move should stop the opponent from moving forward to prevent the escape. *Lower Left.* To get his other foot off the mat, the wrestler will rotate his hips toward the foot already on the mat. This twisting motion will enable him to get the right foot on the mat. He will then thrust himself upward and at the same time push against his opponent with his back. *Lower Right.* The escape is completed when the wrestler jams his elbow back between him and his opponent. This will clear his hips and allow him to spin around to face his opponent. He will score a point for the escape and will also be in the neutral position. Then he can go for a takedown.

38

side leg. Then, when your foot is on the mat, take your inside arm and turn the palm up. Next jam your elbow back, which will prevent your opponent from moving forward. Then, rotate your hips toward the foot that is on the mat and get your other foot on the mat. Then thrust upward, pushing against your opponent with your back.

Now thrust the same elbow between your body and your opponent. This will clear your hip and you should be able to turn around to face him. That will complete the stand-up and put you right back in the neutral position.

Another basic escape maneuver is the *short sit-out*. The object for the bottom wrestler is to get his legs into a sitting position. The first move is to step up on the outside leg, which is the leg furthest from the opponent. Then quickly slide your inside leg underneath your body and out to come to a sitting position. Now you've got to be careful.

Unless your elbows are tucked in tight to your body, your opponent can easily slip under your arms and hook you back to the mat. If you tuck the elbows and he can't do that, you must decide how to complete the escape. The most popular move is to turn onto your shoulder while controlling your opponent's wrist at your waist. Then kick your outside leg hard over the top. This should help you roll into a position facing your opponent. A quick jump to the feet and you've escaped.

It is also possible to go for a reversal from the sit-out position. Many times, a variety of different roll moves are used. This one is called the *Granby roll*. It starts with the sitting position you reached with the short sit-out. If you finished correctly, you'll still have control of your opponent's hand.

Keep control and with your other arm, push on the mat and raise your hips. Then kick hard across your shoulder with the leg opposite the arm pushing you off the mat. Still holding your

*Top.* Another popular escape move is the short sit-out. To do this, the wrestler in the bottom position begins by stepping out with his outside leg. His goal is to get both legs into a sitting position. *Middle.* To get the second leg out, he must slide his inside leg underneath his body quickly. This will bring him to the sitting position shown here. One thing the wrestler sitting out must remember is to keep his elbows in close to his body. Otherwise, his opponent can hook his arms and throw him back to the mat. So at this point, the escape is still not complete. *Bottom.* One way to complete it is for the wrestler to turn his shoulder down to the mat and kick his outside leg hard over the top. If the wrestler can complete this roll, he will end up in a position facing his opponent. Then, a quick jump to his feet will allow him to score with an escape.

opponent's hand to your waist, roll over from one shoulder to the other. When you complete the roll, you will almost be in a sitting position again. Only this time your opponent will have been rolled to the mat behind you.

Quickly flop to one side and pivot around. That should bring you up behind your opponent. If you can get control, you will be awarded two points for a reversal. Like all the moves described, this one must be done smoothly, but explosively. Any delay, any pause and your opponent can counter or make a reversing move of his own.

There's another escape move that can be used in certain situations. Some call it the *scoot-away*, while others call it the *run-and-tear*. In a sense, it involves running away from your opponent. But not because you're scared. You are again trying to score a point for an escape.

This maneuver can be tried by the bottom man as soon as the command to wrestle is given. First, you make a strong move with your feet, as in the stand-up escape. Only this time you don't lean back into your opponent and attempt to turn and face him. Instead, you lean forward and, while trying to pry your opponent's hands apart, actually begin pulling away from him as hard as you can.

There are times when this maneuver looks like a foot race. One wrestler is almost running, while the other is still trying to grab on to take him back down to the mat. If you can get away, you've earned an escape.

The move makes good sense when the top man moves to try to control your ankle. That puts him a bit further behind you. He now has your waist and ankle, but if you're quick enough, you might be able to scoot away. Let him have the ankle and concentrate on freeing your waist with both hands.

*Left.* The scoot-away escape can be successful only if it is done with an explosive movement. It can be used when the top man goes for an ankle tie up, as shown here. The bottom wrestler begins by bringing his upper body off the mat and tries to clear his waist by freeing himself from his opponent's grasp. *Right.* His waist clear, the wrestler now can try to leap away from his opponent, pushing off on his front foot. The motion should be like that of a sprinter coming out of the starting blocks. In fact, the escaping wrestler should take two leaps to make sure his opponent is not right behind him, ready to throw him back to the mat when he turns. The scoot-away sometimes looks like a foot race, but it can work.

Once your waist is clear, step up with your inside leg and try to explode away, much like a sprinter coming out of the blocks. If your opponent manages to hang on, do it again. This time try to leap away, putting as much distance between you and your opponent as you can. Always take two leaps before you turn. If you turn on the first leap, your opponent may be too close and drive into you. As soon as you're free, start looking for the takedown.

There are two other basic reversals a young wrestler can learn. Both begin in the bottom position, with your opponent at the advantage. The first is usually called the *side roll*. As with all wrestling moves, it must be done very quickly and decisively.

42

At the command to wrestle, you reach up and grab the opponent's hand that is around your waist. As you do this, you begin dropping your body to the side where you have grabbed the hand. The key here is to lift the inside foot to block your opponent's knee. That way, he can't step across your body to counter the roll.

Then you can continue to roll in the same direction. If you do this right, you'll find your opponent beginning to follow over your back. Then raise the foot that has been blocking his knee and this will cause him to continue to be pulled over you. With another strong move, scissor your legs and let them help you pivot over on top of your opponent. You should still have wrist control as you pivot over him. Then you can look for a possible pinning move.

The different types of rolls are basic moves in reversals and escapes, and should be practiced often. Some wrestlers will try to counter a roll with a roll of their own. That is an exciting maneuver to watch.

It is important that each wrestler know how to complete a roll without having it backfire on him. And a good coach can show his wrestlers a number of ways to do this.

One last reversal move from the bottom position is simply called the *switch*. At the whistle, quickly take your outside hand and move it across your body so you're opponent can't grab it. This can lead to a momentary criss-crossing of the hands on the mat.

As your cross the hands, begin pushing your body upward with your outside leg. Then slide the inside leg under your body. That will pivot you into a sitting position. From there, quickly bring your top arm over your opponent's arm and grab the inside of his leg. By moving your hips back and pushing

*Upper Left.* One way not only to escape an opponent, but also to take command with a reversal, is called a side roll. It begins with the bottom wrestler reaching up and grabbing the top man's hand that is around his waist. At the same time, he begins to drop his body to the side where he has grabbed the hand. *Upper Right.* As he drops to the mat, the bottom man must lift his inside foot to block his opponent's knee. This will keep the top man from stepping across to counter the roll. Once the bottom man has the foot in place, he can keep rolling in the same direction. *Lower Left.* When the maneuver is done correctly, the top man will find himself being rolled over the bottom man's back. By raising the foot that was blocking his opponent's knee, the bottom man will keep his opponent rolling and will put himself in position to complete the reversal. *Lower Right.* While still keeping control of his opponent's right wrist, the wrestler completes the side-roll reversal by scissoring his legs. As he does this, he pivots over his opponent and gains control. He is then in a position to attempt a pinning maneuver of his own.

44

down with your shoulder, you can force your opponent's shoulder to the mat.

Once his shoulder is down, you should be able to pivot around and take control on top. As you make the pivot, be sure

*Upper Left.*   Another way to get a reversal is called the switch. The bottom wrestler begins by moving his outside hand across his body so that his opponent cannot grab it. At the same time, he will begin to rise up on his outside leg and be ready to make a quick move with the inside leg. *Upper Right.*   By sliding the inside leg under his body, the wrestler can pivot into a sitting position. Now, if he is quick enough, he can complete the reversal. *Lower Left.*   Next, he must move his hips out and down. This will force his opponent's shoulder to the mat and allow him to make the final move. *Lower Right.*   To pivot and take control, the wrestler must swing his outside leg in a high, wide arc. The high kick will stop his opponent from stepping back over his legs and preventing the reversal.

to kick your outside leg high in a wide arc. This will prevent your opponent from countering with a quick step over your legs as you pivot. If he does that, he can prevent the reversal. But if you kick high and stop him, you've got it.

Here are some basic tips on escapes and reversals. A quick start is very important. If you are going to make a move, start it the second the referee blows the whistle. If you get even a split-second head start on your opponent, there is a better chance that the move will work. Speed and power should be the key ingredients to any move. If you don't move fast enough, you won't make it. And if your move doesn't have enough power behind it, your opponent can counter more easily.

If you try a move and it doesn't work, stop right away. It's better to go immediately to a second move. Don't keep trying one that hasn't worked the first time. No matter what, keep moving. If you stop, even just to get your bearings, your opponent will get an even bigger advantage.

Once again, be determined. If you have the will to escape, you can. Just keep moving faster and harder, and think positively. Then the points will come.

## Learning Breakdowns And Pins

Up to now, we have talked about the bottom man escaping and reversing. This isn't the only thing that can happen when the wrestlers take their positions in the second and third period. The top man doesn't wait around to be a victim. There are moves he can make to keep the advantage and set up a pin. These are called *breakdowns*.

The simplest form of breakdown involves knocking out your opponent's supports and getting him flat to the mat. This means taking away a leg, or both legs. Or an arm, or both arms.

There are a number of ways to do this. Once it's done, the wrestler with the advantage must ride his opponent while trying to work for a pin.

Perhaps the most basic breakdown is the *outside ankle breakdown*, also called an *ankle check*. This is often the first breakdown maneuver young wrestlers will learn. At the whistle, the top man drops his hand from his opponent's waist and quickly grabs the outside ankle. As he does this, he also moves his other hand from his opponent's elbow to the waist. Both of these moves must be done with lightning speed, a split second after the whistle sounds.

The next step is to pick the opponent's ankle off the mat and at the same time step behind it. A hard forward drive with the entire body will push the opponent to the mat. Finally, a step up with the outside leg will lock the ankle of the other man. The top wrestler now has control and can ride while trying for a pinning move.

*Left.* **The outside-ankle breakdown is a very basic move from the top position. Begin by shifting your hand from your opponent's waist to his outside ankle. At the same time, take your other hand off your opponent's elbow and move it to his waist.** *Right.* **When these two quick moves have been made, you can complete the breakdown by picking up your opponent's ankle. Then, using your foot for power, push forward and drive him to the mat.**

47

A similar breakdown involves grabbing the opposite ankle. This time, the top man drops his hand off his opponent's elbow to grab the inside ankle. His other arm remains around his opponent's waist. Now it's just a matter of picking up the inside ankle and driving foward. When the bottom man hits the mat, the top man steps up once more to lock the ankle.

The *near-arm breakdown* is yet another very basic maneuver that all wrestlers must learn. This time there is no moving out of the starting position. The top man simply pulls back hard on the inside arm of his opponent. At the same time, he uses his back leg to drive into the man, forcing him down to the mat.

Still another breakdown maneuver is the *lace*, or *Navy ride*. At the whistle, the top man takes the arm that is around the bottom man's waist and grabs him under the crotch. As he lifts his man by the crotch, he also drives forward, forcing his man to the mat. It's important to move up higher than usual for this move. The top man must have his chest pressing down on the upper shoulders of the bottom man.

A breakdown that can lead right into a pinning maneuver is sometimes called the *head-arm lever breakdown*. With this one, the top man slides his arm down from his opponent's elbow (the starting position) to the wrist. At the same time, he puts his head into the back of his opponent's arm between the arm and shoulder.

The top man can then drive his opponent to the mat by pulling the wrist out and back, and pushing hard with his head. Once again, the breakdown has been completed and the top man is in control. Now he must work for the pin.

Before going on to pins, just a few quick tips on breakdowns. When you start in the top position, always keep your head up to improve your balance. When grabbing an arm, wrist or ankle,

*Upper Right.* The inside-ankle breakdown is a similar move, in which the top wrestler releases his grip from the down man's elbow and grabs him by the inside ankle. *Lower Right.* As he lifts the ankle off the mat, the top wrestler drives forward and pushes his opponent to the mat. He then quickly moves forward to lock up the ankle, which completes the breakdown.

*Upper Left.* With the near-arm breakdown, the top man simply pulls back hard on the inside arm of his opponent. He can do this without moving from the starting, or referee's, position. *Lower Left.* From there he uses his back leg to lean hard into his opponent, driving him to the mat for the breakdown.

49

*Left.* The head-arm lever breakdown is a little tougher to learn. But if it is done right, it can take a wrestler right into the pinning position. Starting in the top position, slide the hand on your opponent's elbow down to his wrist. At the same time, put your head into the back of your opponent's arm. Your head should be between his arm and shoulder. *Right.* Once your head is in place, you can drive your opponent to the mat by pushing with your head at the same time you pull his wrist out and back.

always keep the thumb opposite the index finger for a better grip.

Attempt a pinning maneuver as soon as you break down your opponent. Don't just ride with no plan or purpose. If you're aggressive and eager for a pin, your opponent won't have time to work on escapes and reversals. And don't relax. When you have the advantage, always try to finish your opponent off. Otherwise, you might let him off the hook.

There are a number of holds that can result in a pin. Some of them develop from breakdowns, but only if the wrestler knows how to apply them. One of the most popular is the *half nelson*. In fact, it has often been called the most basic of all the wrestling pins.

The half nelson can be applied following an ankle breakdown or the head-arm lever breakdown. To put your opponent into the half nelson, you've got to force one arm over his body and around his waist. The second arm goes under his upper arm and across his head from the back, your elbow behind him.

50

The breakdown complete, you can go for a pinning maneuver. One good way to do this is with the half nelson. Starting in the breakdown position, slide your head under the arm you are controlling. Then lift your head while arching your back. At the same time, kick your bottom leg underneath. This should bring you almost to a sitting position, as shown here.

With your right arm around your opponent's waist, you must swing your left arm over the top and hook him behind the head. Continue to push and drive his back closer to the mat as you move to secure his head. If you let up the pressure for even a second, he may be able to start a countering move.

Once your arm is around his head, you can continue to drive forward, pushing with your legs. You now want to turn your opponent onto his back.

When you have your opponent on his back, you must keep your chest tight against his and your elbow around the back of his head. At this point you have him in the half nelson. Now you can drive forward to try for the pin.

By securing your opponent's head and then driving forward, you can try to turn him onto his back. As you drive, it will help if you lift one of his legs. Once you have the man on his back, your chest should be tight against his, with your elbow far around the back of his head. Then you can try for the pin.

The *bar-arm* is another good move to control, turn and then pin an opponent. It starts with you in control and your opponent on his side, and trying to escape. To get the bar, reach over your opponent's arm at the elbow. Then bring his arm upward and hook under it, putting the palm of your hand across the middle of his back. Use your free arm to block his lower shoulder so he cannot move his body forward to try to escape. When you feel you are in total control, lift the captured arm up high and swing from the outside your hips underneath. Continue to lift the captured arm as you pivot around the front of his head, using your legs to move you and keep you in control.

Once your opponent is nearly on his back, take the arm you used to block the shoulder and swing it behind his head. This part of the grip is similar to the half nelson. With his head and arm under control and your weight on top of him, you have a good chance for the pin.

Another maneuver that can help in controlling your opponent so you can try for a pin is the *cradle*. This is a hold in which you control your opponent by locking your arms around his head and legs. The hands can be locked in three basic ways. With the *wrestler's grip*, the four fingers of one hand face inward and grab the four fingers of the other hand, which face outward.

The *palm lock* has the palms of both hands pressed together with the fingers wrapped tightly around the backs of the hands. The *hands on wrist* grip is just as it sounds. One hand grips the wrist of the other. All three cradle grips can be used. It just depends on which one you feel most comfortable with. But

Another pinning maneuver that involves turning your opponent is the bar-arm pin. This maneuver can be used when you are in control and your opponent is on his side, trying to escape. To begin, you must get his arm in the bar. You do this by reaching over your opponent's arm at the elbow.

Once you hook his arm, bring it upward and push your arm through to place the palm of your hand across the middle of your opponent's back. At the same time, use your free arm to brace yourself and keep your opponent from sliding forward. The free arm is usually placed behind his shoulder.

Continue to raise the captured arm. Then move quickly around his head, pivoting with your feet so you wind up on the other side. If you keep the pressure on your opponent, he should keep moving onto his back as you pivot. Then swing your free arm over the top and secure his head in a way similar to the half nelson.

With your opponent's head and arm under control, put all your weight on him and try to press his shoulders to the mat. This type of pin is often called a "smother" pin.

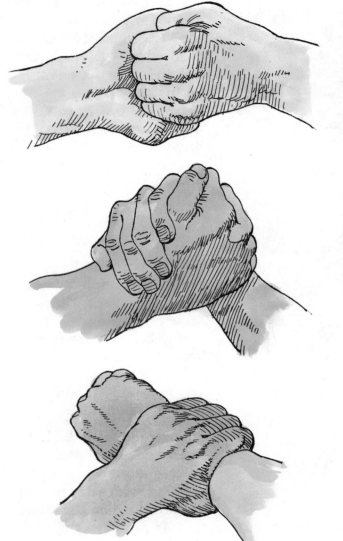

Cradling is a good way to control an opponent. To hold a cradle takes strength, especially in the hands. There are three grips a wrestler can use to lock up a cradle. This one is called the wrestler's grip, with the fingers on each hand interlocked with one another.

Another cradling grip is the palm lock. Here the wrestler's palms are pressed together, the fingers wrapped tightly around the backs of the hands.

The hands-on-wrist grip is the third way to lock up a cradle. One hand simply grabs the opposite wrist to secure the grip.

strong hands definitely help when locking up an opponent with a cradle. And a cradle can definitely lead to a pin.

If you are the top man, you can use the *back cradle* as a counter to a bottom man who tries a sit-out. As the "down" wrestler sits out, you should move with him quickly to push on his upper body and drive his head toward the mat. Then move off to the left side of the man (you can also do it from the right side), and put your right elbow behind his neck. Next grab the elbow of his near arm and pull it across his chest.

54

Now for the cradle. With your left arm, go under his near leg and bring your hands together. Use one of the grips just described. Then, by pushing your right leg tight against his buttocks, you can pull back and maneuver him over your leg. As his hips come off the mat while rolling over your leg, you should have his shoulders close to a pinning position. And you should still have the cradle locked in place.

A cradle maneuver can also help when the bottom man tries to stand out. If he tries to step up with an inside leg and his head is near the leg, then you can use a *near side cradle*. First put your left elbow around his head with your elbow joint on the back of his neck. Your head should be pressed against his side, not over his back.

Then take your right hand off his waist and reach between his knees. You should be able to lock your hands in front of his chest. Once you have the cradle in place, make sure his head stays down. He may try to force it up and sit out. If you apply pressure toward yourself and down at the same time, he won't be able to sit.

If you step up with your rear leg, you should be able to circle and drive and still keep his head down. As you circle, look for a chance to drive him onto his back to set up a pin.

If, however, he tries to stand up with his far leg, then the move is slightly different. The *far side cradle* must be used. First, make sure that your opponent's head is down. Once again, your elbow goes around his head and the waist hand locks around his far knee. As you did before, lock the cradle in front of your opponent's chest.

With the far side cradle, you can go for the pin by rolling under your opponent and then pulling him onto his shoulders. To do this, the cradle must stay tightly locked. Then you must put your knee to the mat on the side to which you are rolling.

*Left.* The far-side cradle is often used when the bottom man tries to step up with his outside leg but leaves his head down. To lock up the cradle, the top wrestler has brought his left hand over his opponent's shoulder and his right hand under the opponent's right knee. The cradle is locked in front of the chest. *Right.* From the far side cradle position, the top man can go for the pin by rolling under his opponent, then pulling him up and onto his shoulders. The move must be quick and the cradle locked tight. As with all wrestling moves, it takes practice.

Your knee must be close to your opponent's knee. This will keep him from moving his knee out to brace himself. If you move quickly and with force, you'll have a good chance to make the roll.

There are many other pinning moves and maneuvers that can lead to a pin. Some your coach will teach you. Others you may learn for yourself while you're on the mat. A wrestler with good instincts will often sense the right thing to do. These basic moves are meant to give a beginner tips about balance and control.

In addition, there is a counter move for almost every move a wrestler tries. Sometimes it depends on which wrestler has better technique. Sometimes it's a matter of speed. Sometimes balance. Sometimes strength. But the more you know, the more things you will be able to try.

# A Word About
# Defensive Wrestling

As mentioned earlier, a wrestler must always be aggressive. He must always be on the attack, trying to score points. But points aren't always enough. While trying to score points, he must also look for the pin. If he gets a fall, the match is over and he doesn't have to worry about points.

But there are times when a wrestler has to go on the defense. If he is in a hold that could lead to a pin, he must try to get himself into a better position. This doesn't always mean attacking. Sometimes he must wrestle defensively. Hopefully, it will only be for a short amount of time.

If a wrestler finds himself on his back, he is in trouble. First of all, there is no way he can attack from that position. Secondly, wrestling while you are on your back is difficult even if you are an experienced grappler.

Every wrestler should know how to get off his back. He has to know how to get out of cradles, a half nelson and other holds that put him onto his back. These are situations that no wrestler can escape with one quick move.

To begin with, a wrestler must have a very strong neck. This will allow him to push his upper body off the mat. It's a maneuver called "bridging." It can start the step-by-step process for a wrestler to get off his back.

He can begin by neck-and-shoulder bridging from one side and then the other. For example, he can start by using his neck to raise his right shoulder off the back. Then, as he comes down, he should try to get an arm between himself and the man on top of him. After a second bridge, maybe both arms will be in between.

It is important for a wrestler to know how to bridge. It is a way he can get his upper body off the mat and avoid a fall or near fall. To bridge correctly, a wrestler must have a very strong neck. Otherwise, bridging like this can be dangerous. Your coach can show you exercises to build the neck muscles, and bridging must be practiced quite often. Used properly, it can sometimes save you from a defeat.

But the real trick of the bridging is for the wrestler to try to turn onto his stomach. He may have to do this a little at a time. The reason the bottom man tries to wedge his arms between himself and the top man to to make it harder for the top man to keep full pressure on the hold. And each bridge and move will get the bottom man off his back and change the angle of the hold.

This is very hard work. But it is worth it because if you don't get out, you might find yourself pinned.

Cradles, also, can put a wrestler in a tough spot. A strong wrestler with his arms locked can really tie his opponent up. And many times a cradle will take away leg and back power, because it forces the head and the knee close together.

The first way to try to break a cradle is to expand your body. Begin stretching your arms and neck, causing the cradle to begin to open. That puts more pressure on your opponent's locked hands. The object is to get your knees and legs as far away from your head as possible. If you can manage this expansion until your opponent's hands can no longer touch, then the cradle is broken.

The above method is almost an inch-by-inch escape. But sometimes, you can break a cradle with one powerful, explosive motion. This can be especially useful if you are being held on your side. It takes great strength, but here's what you do.

Try to hook either the instep or toe of your cradled leg with your free leg. Then place a hand (try to make it the hand nearest the mat) on the knee of the controlled, or cradled, leg. Then put the other arm on top of the first hand. The movement will be to pull down with the free leg and push with both hands.

When everything feels just right, explode. Pull the controlled leg downward with the free leg. At the same time push on the knee with both hands and try to straighten your back. If the leverage is right and you're strong enough, you may break right out of the cradle.

## What It Takes To Win

Wrestling is a very complex sport. The object is simple enough. Two wrestlers go hand-to-hand against each other, with the object being for one to pin the other's shoulders to the mat. But there are so many ways to do this that they cannot all be covered in a book for beginners. Instead, this book has tried to give the newcomer some of the basics of the sport.

That includes what it takes to get ready to be a wrestler and what it takes to win. Unlike some other sports, wrestling is not an activity you can do once a week for fun and exercise. Rather, it's a sport that not only asks for a total commitment. It demands one.

A wrestler must be dedicated. That means working at it and

training for the entire year. During the off season, a wrestler must work to get stronger through weight training. Strength is very important. So is stamina and quickness. A young athlete must always be working to improve himself in all these areas.

In addition, a wrestler must have a very positive outlook. He can't hide a bad day by hoping the ball doesn't come his way, or waiting for his teammates to pick up the slack. He's out there by himself and if he loses his confidence, he's done. He must always think he is going to win. And that means looking for the pin and piling up points along the way.

The wrestler also has to concentrate at all times. He must focus on his opponent and the job to be done. He cannot be aware of anything happening off that mat. If he loses concentration, he is likely to lose the match.

These are all good habits that come out of training and practice. Training must be hard. A set routine is a must. A good coach will know how to balance weight training, drills for quickness and agility, and learning and practicing new holds and maneuvers.

Each takedown, reversal, escape, cradle and pinning combination must be practiced over and over again. Members of a wrestling team spend many hours going up against one another in fierce competition. That's why it's important to have several wrestlers at the same weight class. Only the best one can wrestle. But if one, two, or three teammates are looking for that spot, the competition will be good for everyone.

Many coaches conduct wrestle-offs in the final practice session before a meet. The winners of the wrestle-offs at each weight class will be the ones who compete for the team. The better the competition among teammates, the better all the members of the team will become.

One other word about wrestling. Though it is a hard sport, there are certain rules that are always observed. Wrestlers must conduct themselves as gentleman. There are always handshakes before and after a match. And a wrestler never argues with the referee. His decision is final.

Rarely will you see any display of poor sportsmanship. Throwing headgear, cursing or any disrespect to opposing wrestlers or coaches can result in a default. That's worth six points to the other team, which helps to control a lot of tempers.

So there is a kind of dignity about this competitive sport that makes it different. Wrestling may not be for everyone. But if you want to try it, go ahead. Work hard and learn all you can. If you stick with it, you may someday be a champion. If not, you will still be a better person for trying.

# Glossary

**Bottom position**  The position of a wrestler when he starts a period with both his hands and knees on the mat. It is also called the down position and is considered the position of disadvantage.

**Breakdown**  A maneuver that results in a wrestler losing his support (his arms and legs) and being taken flat to the mat It is usually the one in the bottom position.

**Bridging**  A strength move in which the shoulders and back are raised off the mat by pressing hard with the back of the head and neck. The elbows and feet can also be used to create a bridge.

**Control**  Term used to describe the position of a wrestler who has his opponent restrained and unable to move. This gives him a clear advantage.

**Counter**  A move by a wrestler to stop or reverse an attacking maneuver by his opponent. He can stop the maneuver from working and even get a reversal from his counter.

**Cradle**  A manuever in which a wrestler locks his opponent's head and legs in his arms. This prevents the opponent from moving and often leads to a pin.

**Escape**  A scoring move in which a wrestler frees himself from the control of his opponent. It is worth one point.

**Fall**  Another term for a pin, in which a wrestler holds his opponent's shoulders to the mat, ending the match. A pin must be held for one second in college and two seconds in high school wrestling.

**Freestyle wrestling**  Popular style of wrestling used in high school and colleges. In this style, both the arms and legs can be used in securing and escaping from holds.

**Greco-Roman wrestling**  Style of wrestling in which the wrestler cannot use his feet or legs to secure a hold and cannot apply a hold below an opponent's waist. Greco-Roman and freestyle wrestling are separate Olympic events.

**Illegal hold**  A hold not in the rulebook or one that can injure an opponent, such as a full nelson. The referee will stop a match as soon as he sees an illegal hold.

**Major decision**  A wrestling match that is decided by a difference of 12 to 14 points.

**Match tough**  Expression that applies to an experienced wrestler. He is used to the pressures of tough competition and will not rattle or lose his concentration.

**Near fall**  A scoring situation in which a wrestler has his opponent's shoulders near the mat. Because it can lead to a fall or pin, it is worth two or three points.

**Palm lock**  One method used to lock up

a cradle. The palms of both hands are pressed tightly together with the fingers wrapped around the tops of the hands.

**Penetration** A term used to describe a wrestler driving through his opponent's defenses. Usually used when both wrestlers are facing each other in a standing position.

**Pin** Another term for a fall.

**Predicament** A scoring situation in which a wrestler controls his opponent to the point where the referee feels a fall or near fall may occur. It is worth two points.

**Ready stance** Stance used when both wrestlers are standing in the up position. Feet are spread, knees bent, hands held out in front ready for action.

**Referee's position** Term used to describe an alternative starting position for both the second and third periods. Both wrestlers are on the mat, one in the top and the other in the bottom position.

**Reps** Short for repetitions. Weight training term used to describe how many times a particular exercise is repeated.

**Reversal** Scoring maneuver in which a wrestler not only frees himself from the control of his opponent, but also takes control. It is worth two points.

**Riding time** The total amount of time one wrestler controls the other. There is a point awarded in college wrestling for each minute of riding time. There are no points awarded for riding time in high school wrestling.

**Set** Weight training term for the total number of reps used in an exercise. Depending on the exercise and its pur-

pose, five, ten, or 15 reps can equal one set.

**Shooting** Terms used to describe a quick move in which one wrestler dives or lunges at his opponent's feet.

**Singlet** The name of the one-piece uniform worn by wrestlers. It consists of shorts and an attached top.

**Stalling** The failure of a wrestler to be aggressive. After a warning, a penalty point may be given to his opponent.

**Superior decision** A wrestling match that is decided by a difference of 12 or more points.

**Takedown** A scoring maneuver in which one wrestler takes his opponent to the mat from the neutral, or standing, position. It is worth two points.

**Technical fall** Term used for the ending of a wrestling match when one wrestler has built a 15-point lead over his opponent. The match ends as soon as the 15-point lead is achieved, no matter at what point in the match.

**Tie up** The interlocking of hands or arms from the neutral position in an attempt to get a takedown.

**Top position** The position of advantage that can begin the second and/or third periods. The top man is above and behind his opponent. He places an arm around his opponent's waist and puts his other hand loosely on his opponent's elbow.

**Wrestler's grip** Another way to lock up a cradle. The wrestler curls the fingers of both hands around each other and squeezes tightly so that his hands cannot be easily separated.